The Ultimate Self-Teaching Method!

Play Guitar Today!

by Jeff Schroedl and Doug Downing

A Complete Guide to the Basics

Contents

PLAYBACK+
Speed • Pitch • Balance • Loop

To access audio visit:
www.halleonard.com/mylibrary

1205-2661-6286-3827

Track 1

Introduction

Welcome to Book 2 of *Play Guitar Today!*, the series designed to prepare you for any style of guitar playing. Whatever your taste in music—rock, blues, jazz, classical—*Play Guitar Today!* will give you the start you need.

In Book 1, we covered the basics of music and of the guitar. In Book 2, we'll really expand on that knowledge. We'll learn new chords, strumming patterns, and playing techniques. We'll even learn how to play higher up on the guitar neck. We'll explore a variety of essential tools that will prepare you for any style of guitar playing. As always, you'll be accompanied by a band on most songs, making learning to play guitar enjoyable and easy.

Recording Credits: Todd Greene, Producer; Jake Johnson, Engineer;
Doug Boduch, Guitar; Scott Schroedl, Drums; Tom McGirr, Bass; Warren Wiegratz, Keyboards; Andy Dress, Narration

ISBN 978-0-634-00409-4

Visit Hal Leonard Online at
www.halleonard.com

World headquarters, contact:
Hal Leonard
7777 West Bluemound Road
Milwaukee, WI 53213
Email: info@halleonard.com

In Europe, contact:
Hal Leonard Europe Limited
Dettingen Way
Bury St Edmunds, Suffolk, IP33 3YB
Email: info@halleonardeurope.com

In Australia, contact:
Hal Leonard Australia Pty. Ltd.
4 Lentara Court
Cheltenham, Victoria, 3192 Australia
Email: info@halleonard.com.au

T0045631

Tuning Your Guitar

The guitar's six open strings should be tuned to the pitches E–A–D–G–B–E (low to high). These can be found on track 2, or from one of the following sources:

The Piano

If you have a piano or keyboard, play each note shown one at a time, and tune each guitar string to matches its corresponding pitch.

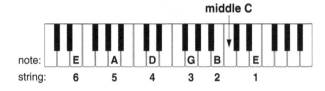

A Pitch Pipe

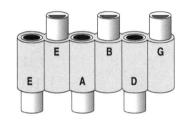

A pitch pipe, available from most music stores, may also be used to find these pitches.

An Electronic Tuner

An electronic tuner will "listen" to the sound of each string as you play it and indicate whether the pitch is too high or too low. You should adjust each string accordingly.

Relative Tuning

Whichever source you use, always check your tuning with the following method:

1.   Tune the 6th string E to a piano, a pitch pipe, an electronic tuner, or the audio. If none of these are available, approximate E as best you can.

2.   Press the 6th string at the 5th fret. This is A. Tune the open 5th string to this pitch.

3.   Press the 5th string at the 5th fret. This is D. Tune the open 4th string to this pitch.

4.   Press the 4th string at the 5th fret. This is G. Tune the open 3rd string to this pitch.

5.   Press the 3rd string at the 4th fret. This is B. Tune the open 2nd string to this pitch.

6.   Press the 2nd string at the 5th fret. This is E. Tune the open 1st string to this pitch.

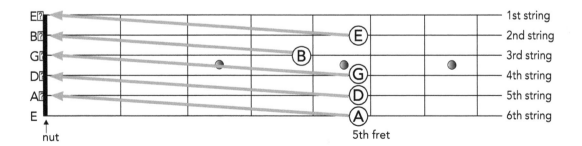

This is called *relative tuning* because the strings are tuned relative to one another. It's a great way to tune your guitar when no pitch sources are available.

Movable Power Chords

Track 3

Power chords are probably the easiest type of chord to play on the guitar, and they're very common to rock and pop styles. In Book 1, we learned three open-position power chords: E5, A5, and D5. Now, with just one more shape, we can learn to play any power chord, anywhere along the neck...

The Two-Note Shape

This shape isn't labeled with a chord name because it's **movable**—that is, you can play it anywhere up or down the neck, and you'll get a different chord. You can base it off of the sixth string, or off of the fifth string.

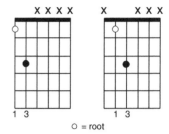

○ = root

Go ahead: pick any note along the fifth or sixth string, and apply this shape to it. The name of the power chord you're playing will always be the root (the lowest note) plus the suffix "5." For example, if you start on F, you get an F5 power chord. If you start on C, you get a C5 power chord, and so on. Here are a few examples for you to get your hands on:

▶ Notice that some power chords, like B♭5, can be played on either the 5th or the 6th string.

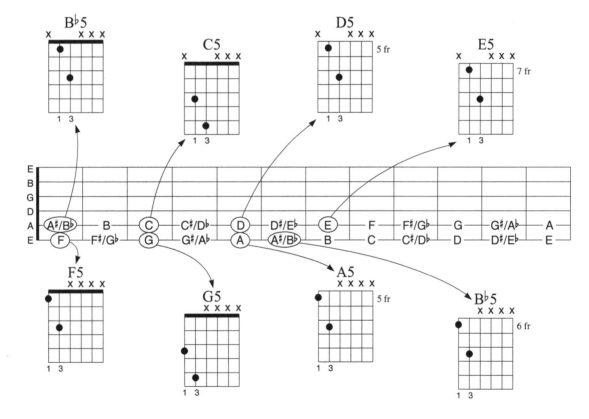

Track 4

Power Play

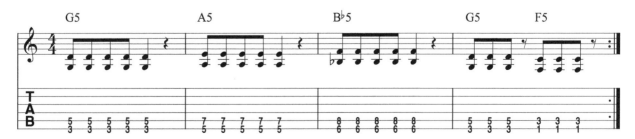

Here are a few songs that move between strings 5 and 6.

Track 5

'50s Pop

Track 6

'60s Rock

To keep
your left
hand from
cramping,
try releasing
it slightly
as you slide
from one
power chord
to the next.

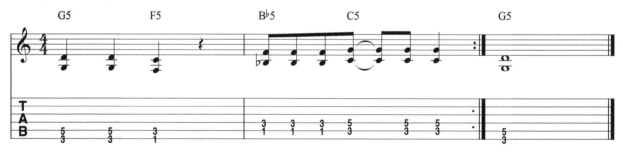

Track 7

'70s Heavy

Muting the Upper Strings

To keep unwanted strings from sounding when playing power chords, let your first finger lay across the upper strings lightly. For power chords along the fifth string, allow your fingertip to mute the sixth string as well, as shown.

4

Track 8

'80s Rock

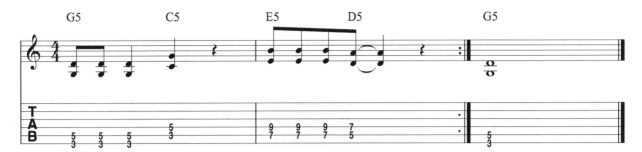

The Three-Note Shape

Just in case you're interested, here's another option for playing power chords.

This **three-note shape** sounds a little fuller than the two-note version. Otherwise, it's pretty much the same chord. You can use it anywhere along the neck, on the sixth string or the fifth string.

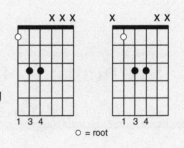

○ = root

Track 9

'90s Alternative

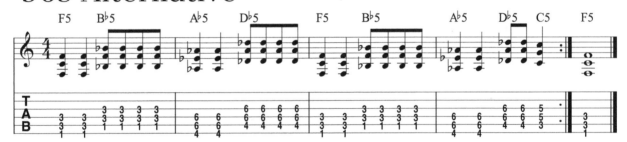

Palm Muting

Palm muting is a special technique in which you allow the side or heel of your picking hand to rest against the bridge, muffling or "muting" the strings as you play. Use this technique when you see the abbreviation "P.M." under the notes (between the staff and TAB).

Track 10

Ridin' Down the Highway

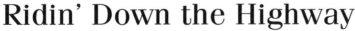

An *accent mark* (>) written above or below a note or chord means you should play that note or chord slightly louder than the others.

Track 11

Thick Groove

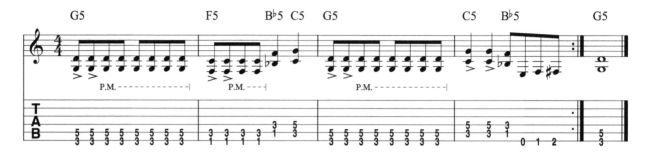

Sixteenth Notes and Rests

Sixteenth notes look like eighth notes, but they have two flags or beams:

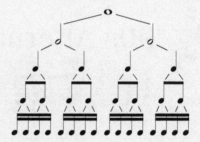

Sixteenth rests also have two flags:

Two sixteenths equal one eighth. Four sixteenths equal one quarter. Here's a diagram showing the relationship of sixteenth notes to all the rhythmic values you've learned:

To help you keep track of the beat, consecutive sixteenth notes are connected with a beam. To count sixteenths, divide the beat into four, and count "1-e-&-a, 2-e-&-a, 3-e-&-a, 4-e-&-a":

1 e & a 2 e & a 3 e & a 4 e & a

To help you get a feel for sixteenth notes, listen to the following track, then try playing along.

Track 12

Faster, Please

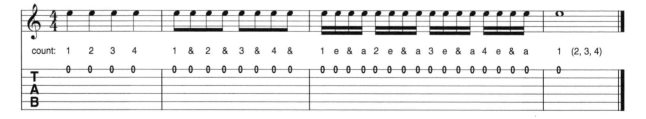

Because sixteenths move so quickly, you'll find them easier to play if you alternate downstrokes (⊓) with upstrokes (V). Try that on this example.

Alternate Sixteenths

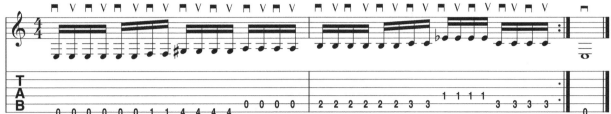

Now try sixteenths with a few power chords. Stick with just downstrokes on this one.

Power Sixteenths

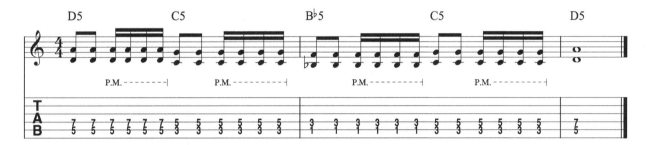

Of course, you can apply the sixteenth rhythm to open chords as well. Try alternate strumming (downstrokes and upstrokes) with these chords from Book 1:

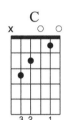  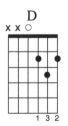  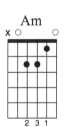 

Open Chord Strumming

► Tap your foot once for each quarter note, even though you're counting (and playing) in sixteenths.

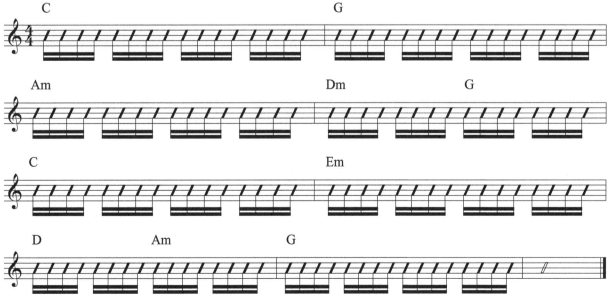

7

LESSON 2 | New Open Chords

Track 16

Open chords are chords that contain one or more open strings; they are the most fundamental chords to all styles of guitar playing. In Book 1, we learned several open chords: C, G, D, Em, Am, and Dm. Now we'll add a few more.

E

■ The open E chord is similar to Em, but you add your first finger on the third string.

A

■ This open A chord is a little bit like Am, but notice that all three fingers belong on the second fret.

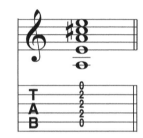

Try switching between E major and minor; then, between A major and minor.

Track 17

Major to Minor

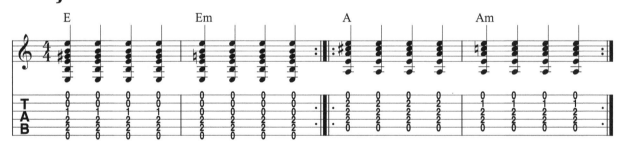

Track 18

Simple Strumming

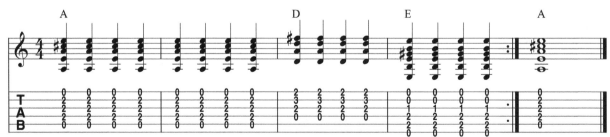

If your fingers feel too crowded on the A chord, consider an option many electric guitarists use: Flatten your first finger at the first joint, laying it across strings 2–4.

Sometimes, what chord you play isn't as important as how you play it. Let's look at a few easy strumming patterns. Play close attention to the stroke indications (⊓ and V).

Strum pattern #1

This one works great at almost any tempo.

Track 19

Strum, Strum, Strum!

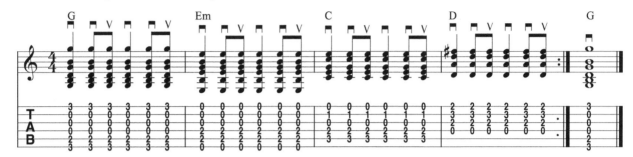

Strum pattern #2

Try this one with medium to faster-tempo songs.

Track 20

Unplugged and Strumming

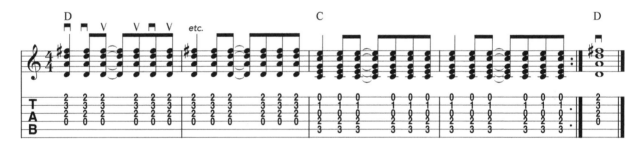

The "Open Strum"

Shifting between chords while strumming continuous eighth notes can be tough! One trick that many guitarists use is the "open strum." The basic idea is this: On the last eighth note before a chord change, let go of the previous chord and begin getting your fingers in place for the next one—*while your right hand strums the open strings.*

Track 21

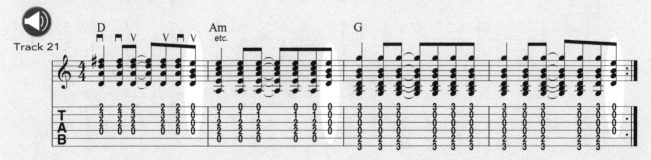

This should give you just enough time to grab that next chord, without having to slow down or skip a beat in your strumming.

Strum pattern #3

This one uses sixteenth notes and works best with slower tempo songs.

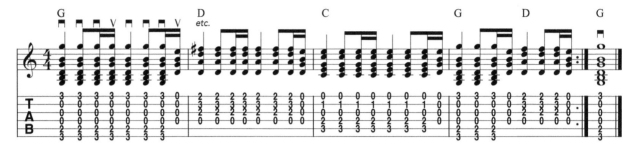

Track 22

Ballad

Strum pattern #4

Here are a few for 3/4 meter.

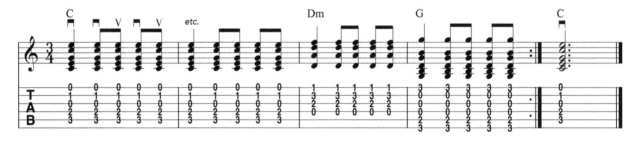

Track 23

Waltz for Bink

The more you play guitar, the more you'll be able to sense when to play on the beat or between beats, and when to change rhythm patterns. Notice how the strumming pattern changes from measure to measure in this next example. (Pay close attention to the downstrokes and upstrokes.)

Track 24

That's What I Like

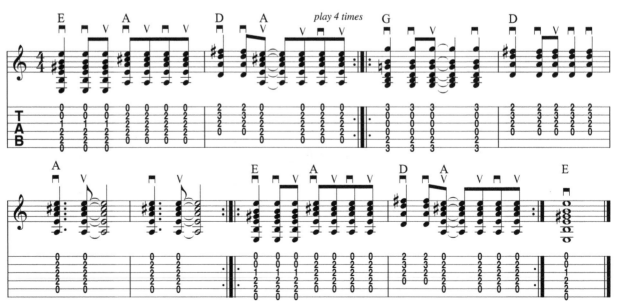

Here's another type of muting effect that can add accent and variety to your strumming patterns. Try this: while strumming a chord with your right hand, let the heel or side of your palm hit the strings a split second before you strike them with your pick. The result should be a muffled, percussive sound (indicated with an "x" in notation and TAB).

Track 25

The Muted Strum

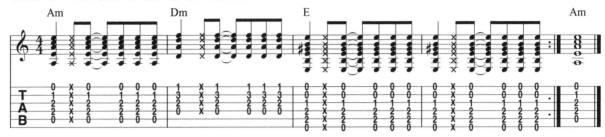

Here's a tip: With your right hand resting on the strings, the strumming motion will actually come from your wrist. It may take you a few tries to get this, so be patient. Also, don't forget to release your hand for the following upstroke!

One More Chord: F

F major requires a new technique—the use of a *barre* (pronounced "bar"). Barring is done by flattening a finger across more than one string at a time.

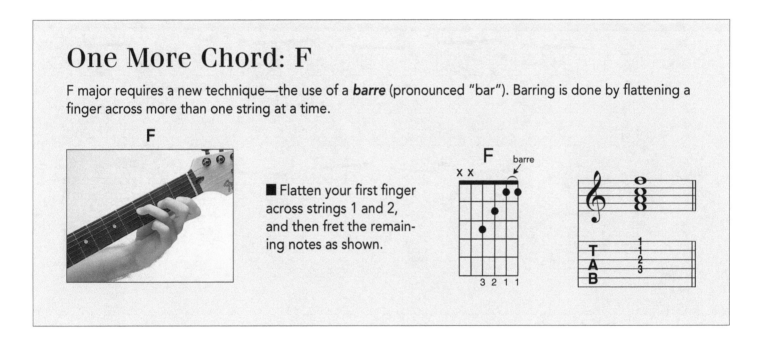

■ Flatten your first finger across strings 1 and 2, and then fret the remaining notes as shown.

The toughest part here will be getting both notes of your barre to sound cleanly. If the chord sounds bad, play each string one at a time, then readjust your barring finger if you need to.

Track 26

Country Life

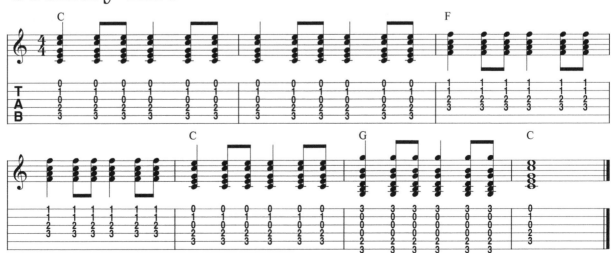

Barring comes in very handy, as we'll see later on. So practice this technique until it comes naturally.

Track 27

The Shape of Things to Come

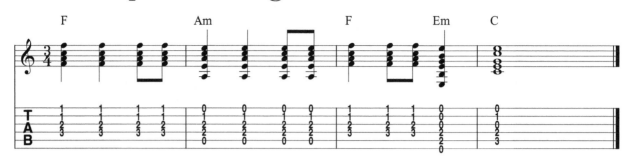

Arpeggios (a.k.a. Broken Chords)

Strumming isn't your only option when playing chords; another way to play chords is by picking them, one note at a time. *Arpeggios* (or *broken chords*) offer a lighter accompanimental approach. They work nicely for ballads—or just about any style, really.

Track 28

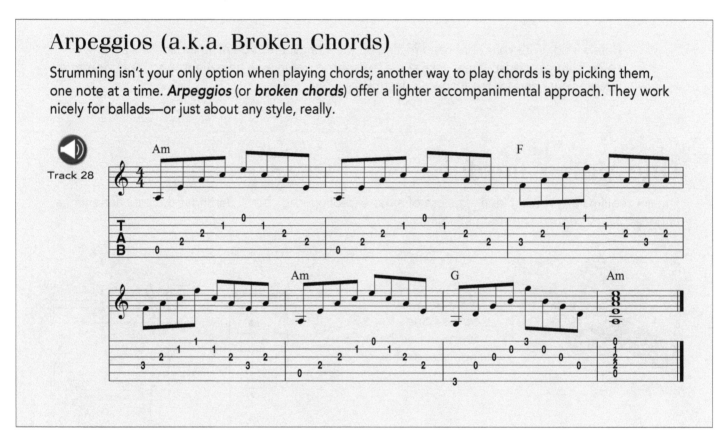

One advantage of arpeggios is that they give you more time to fret each chord—technically, you only need to lay down one finger at a time.

Note by Note

Track 29

► Once each finger is in place, hold it there for the duration of the chord.

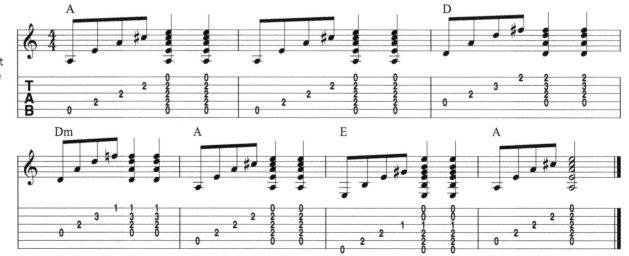

LESSON 3 | First Position Review

Track 30

Let's take some time to review the notes that we learned in Book 1. This area of the guitar neck is known as *first position*.

Notice that some frets seem to have two different note names, like F♯ and G♭? These are called *enharmonic equivalents*—two different note names for the same pitch. Either spelling is acceptable.

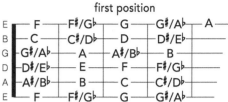

*This note can also be played on the third string, fourth fret.

Remember: in general, we follow the *one-finger-per-fret* rule—first finger on the first fret, second finger on the second fret, and so on. The exception is the high A, which can be played by sliding the pinky up to the fifth fret.

The Road to Glory

Track 31

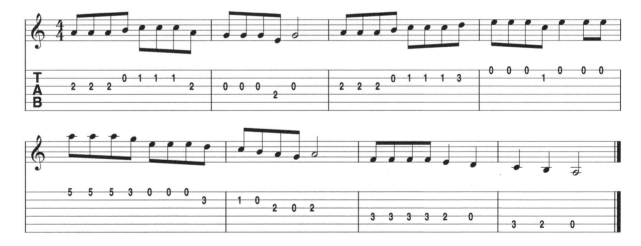

Syncopation

Track 32

▶ Playing notes "off the beat" is a way of adding rhythmic interest to a melody or riff.

This song has a *1st and 2nd ending* (indicated by brackets and the numbers "1" and "2"). When you finish the 1st ending, return to the initial repeat sign (‖:) and continue. The second time through, skip the 1st ending and jump to the 2nd ending, playing until the end of the song.

Star-Spangled Banner

► A *fermata* sign (⌢) tells you to hold a note for longer than its full value.

Think Chordally!

Sometimes, a melody will force you to stray from the one-finger-per-fret rule—for instance, if there are two notes, one right after another, on different strings but the same fret. In order to play such a line smoothly and connectedly, you'll need to use a more creative fingering.

Track 34

In the Hall of the Mountain King

In some songs, it's common to see the instruction **"let ring."** This simply means that, instead of releasing your fingers after each note is played, you hold them down, allowing the notes to sustain.

Track 35

Estudio

Scales and Keys

Track 36

Now that you've begun to get a handle on the basic materials of music—notes and chords—it's time to start looking at how music is organized. Let's take a look at two very important concepts in music: *scale* and *key*.

What's a Scale?

A scale is a series of notes used to create a melody, a solo, or a lick. Two things give a scale its name: the scale's **root** (the lowest note), and its **quality**, which is determined by the pattern of whole steps and half steps it follows.

Here's a look at the two most important scale qualities:

The Major Scale

The root note here is C, and the quality is major, so this is a C major scale.

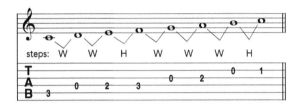

The Minor Scale

The root here is C, but the pattern of whole and half steps makes it a C minor scale.

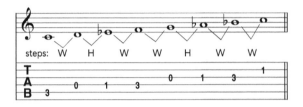

Remember: from one fret to the next on your guitar equals one half step (H); two frets equal a whole step (W).

What's a Key?

When we see that a the notes of a particular song come from a certain scale, we say that the song is **in the key of** that scale. For instance, if the notes of a song all come from the C major scale, we say that the song is in the key of C major.

Try playing through the above C major scale, but change the order of the notes. Begin and end your improvisation on the note C. Notice how the scale seems to be "at rest" when you arrive at C? This is because the note C is the root, or **tonic**—the note around which the key revolves.

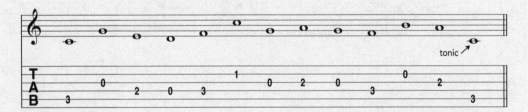

Most scales and keys—except for C major and A minor—contain sharped or flatted notes. Instead of writing these out as they occur, a **key signature** is used at the beginning of each line of music to tell you:

- What notes should be played sharp or flat throughout a song.
- The song's key

For example, the key of G major contains F♯, so its key signature will have or sharp on the F-line. This tells you to play all Fs as F♯ (unless, of course, you see a natural sign ♮.)

key signature

Let's look at some common *major* scales and keys...

Key of C

Based on the C major scale, which has no sharps or flats:

Track 37

Simple Gifts

► "Simple Gifts" is in the key of C; the notes in the song all come from the C major scale.

Key of G

Based on the G major scale, which has one sharp, F♯:

Track 38

Jamaica Farewell

17

Key of F

Based on the F major scale, which has one flat, B♭:

Sweet Sunny South

Track 39

Key of D	Key of A	Key of B♭

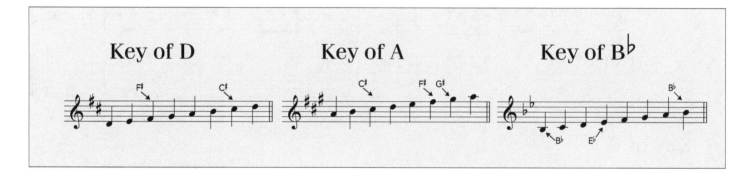

Transposition

Sometimes, you'll find a song that's written either too high or too low for you to sing or play. The solution is to play the song in a different key—one that's more comfortable. Changing the key of a song like this is called *transposition*. Try playing the following simple tune—"Yankee Doodle"—in the keys below. The transposition has already been done for you.

Track 40

New Chords: Dominant 7ths

Keys can also be defined by the chords of a song, and one of the most tell-tale chords is the dominant seventh. Get your fingers on these dominant seventh chords and listen to their sound.

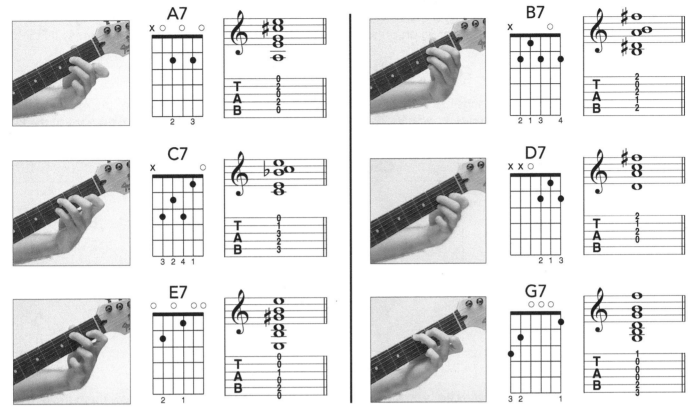

Notice how these chords sound "unresolved?" A dominant chord adds a bit of musical "tension" and makes the ear want "relief." This relief can come from a major or minor chord played after the dominant chord, as in this example:

Track 41

Seventh Heaven

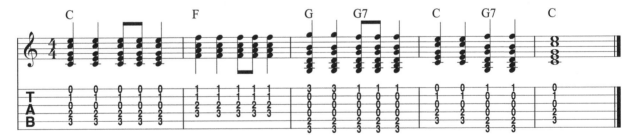

Track 42

Bluesy Seventhis

► Some songs sort of "leave you hanging" by never resolving the dominant chord.

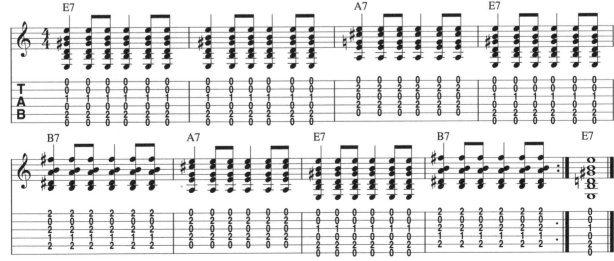

The Blues

Track 43

There are many different styles of music—rock, pop, country, classical, jazz, and so on. Blues is one style of music that's very popular, and it's fun to learn. What is *blues*? Well, like any style, blues is characterized by the chords, progressions, and scales it uses, as well as what forms they all fit into.

The I, IV, and V Chords

Generally, blues songs use only three chords: the first, fourth, and fifth chords of the key (indicated with Roman numerals I, IV, and V). To find these chords, count up the scale from the root of the key:

Key	Chord / Scale Tone							
	I			**IV**	**V**			
Blues in "C"	C	D	E	F	G	A	B	C
Blues in "F"	F	G	A	B♭	C	D	E	F
Blues in "G"	G	A	B	C	D	E	F#	G
Blues in "D"	D	E	F#	G	A	B	C#	D
Blues in "A"	A	B	C#	D	E	F#	G#	A
Blues in "E"	E	F#	G#	A	B	C#	D#	E

The I, IV, and V chords are actually common to all styles of music (so get to know them!). Often, the V chord is played as a dominant seventh chord—like G7, C7, D7, etc.—instead of as a major chord.

The 12-Bar Form

Part of what makes blues unique is that it uses the I, IV, and V chords in a very predictable sequence. The most common is the 12-bar form. This doesn't mean that the song is only 12 bars (or measures) long. Rather, it uses one or more 12-bar phrases, which repeat over and over.

Track 44

Blues in C

▶ Remember *slash notation*? It tells you how many beats each chord is played. Vary your strum patterns.

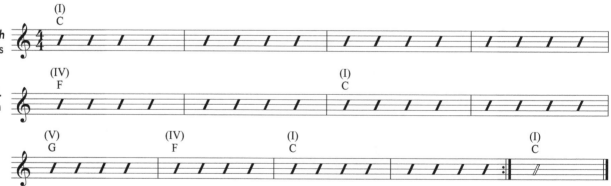

Notice the number of measures that each chord is played. This is the most common 12-bar blues progression. It can be transposed to any key, and it will still sound like the blues.

The last two measures of the 12-bar form are sometimes called the *turnaround*—since they "turn" the form back "around" to the beginning. Musicians sometimes vary the *turnaround*, using different chords or even a riff.

The most common variation is to add a V chord in the very last measure:

Track 45

Blues in G

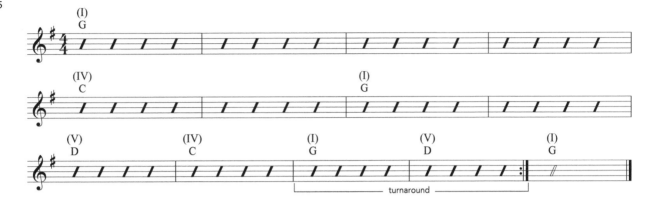

Minor chords are also very popular in blues progressions. This track has a "rock" feel.

Track 46

Minor Blues

The use of all dominant sevenths is another option unique to the blues. (In most other styles, the dominant seventh is reserved for the V chord only.)

Track 47

Seventh Chord Blues

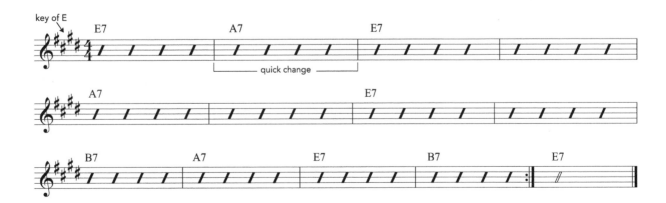

See the IV chord in measure 2? This is called a *quick change*, since you "change" to the IV and "quickly" return to the I.

Blues progressions don't necessarily require full chords. The following blues-based "back and forth" rhythm was made popular by Chuck Berry and other early rock 'n' roll players.

Track 48

Berry Pickin'

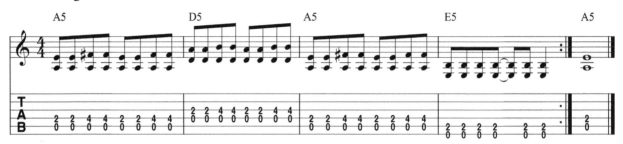

Moving Up the Neck

The "back-and-forth" rhythm can be applied to movable power chords fairly easily. First, play a two-note movable power chord, then keep your fingers in the same shape and add your pinky two frets above your third finger. You may feel a bit of a stretch, but hang in there.

Track 49

Rockin' Blues

► Also try playing the power chord with your first and second fingers instead, adding your pinky for the top note.

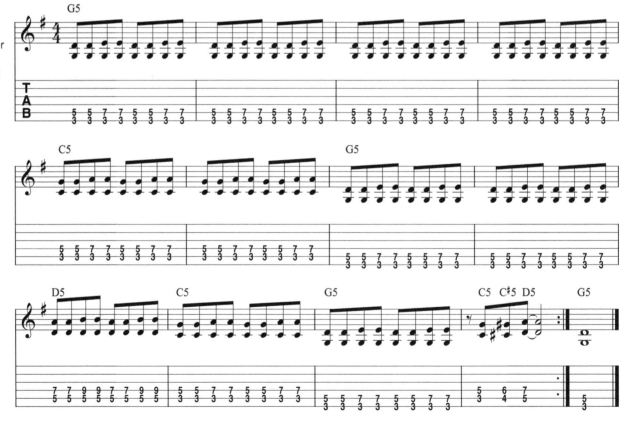

The Blues Scale

If you want to spice up a blues jam, try soloing over a 12-bar section using notes from the blues scale. This scale is actually popular in rock and jazz as well. First, notice the scale's step pattern, then learn its fingering.

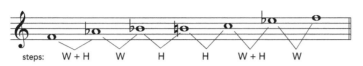

Blues scale (F as root)

Movable fretboard pattern

As with the major and minor scales you learned, the blues scale can be started from any root note. Plus, this particular fretboard pattern is movable—meaning that you can slide it up the neck and start it from any root along the sixth string. Commit it to memory, and use it to form some great riffs and solos like this one:

Track 50

Takin' the Lead

Introducing... The Shuffle Feel

The *shuffle feel* is a very common element of rock, blues, pop, and jazz music. It uses a new rhythmic value called a triplet.

By now, you know that a quarter note divided into two equal parts is two eighth notes. And a quarter note divided into four equal parts is four sixteenth notes. But a quarter note divided into three equal parts? This is an *eighth-note triplet*:

Triplets are beamed together with a number 3. To count a triplet, simply say the word "tri-pl-et" during one beat. Tap your foot to the beat, and count out loud:

count: 1　2　tri - pl - let　4　　tri - pl - let　tri - pl - let　3　4　　1　2　& tri - pl - let　4

23

Shuffle rhythm can be derived from a triplet rhythm by inserting a rest in the middle of the triplet, or by combining the first two eighth notes of the triplet into a quarter. The result is like a triplet with a silent middle eighth note.

Once you get a hang of this "bouncy" feel, you'll never forget it...

Track 51

Chuck's Blues

Shuffle notation can be hard to read. So instead, you'll often see straight eighth notes with the word "swing" or ( ) written at the beginning of the song. This tells you to swing all eighth notes.

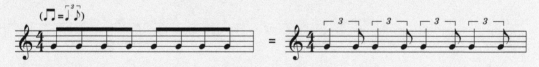

Track 52

Blue Note Shuffle

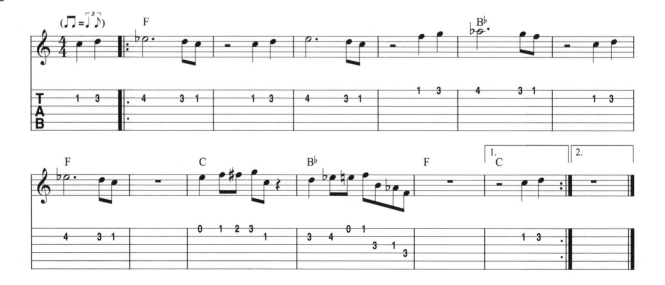

The Fifth Position

Track 53

So far, we've learned to read in the first position of the guitar—a skill that will serve us well in many situations and in many styles of music. But not every song can be played down there, so let's move on up to the *fifth position*.

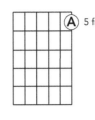

(A) 5 fr

Fifth position starts on the high A at the 5th fret—this time played with the index finger. (Most guitars have a white dot, or other marker, at the 5th fret, which should help you find this position quickly.)

Starting at the 5th fret allows us to access several more notes on the high E string that weren't available to us in first position. Of course, it also gives new fingerings for many familiar notes. Take a few minutes to review the diagram and exercise below.

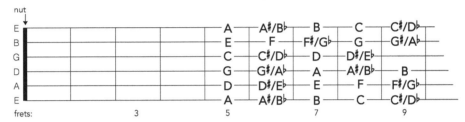

You may notice that, since we no longer have the open strings working for us, we have to cover more frets—in general, follow the one-finger-per-fret rule, but allow your pinky to fret both the 8th and 9th frets.

Fifth Position

▶ Make sure you spend time learning where the notes are both on the fretboard *and* on the staff. (Tell your fingers what you're playing—say each note aloud as you play it.)

*This note can also be played at the third string, fourth fret.

To give you a better feel for this position, try a few scales. This one can be played in open position or fifth, so try it both ways.

A Minor

Track 54

25

C Major

This one takes advantage of new high notes on the first string.

Next, try some riffs in this new position.

Track 56

Hazy Days

Track 57

Blue House

This one uses some open strings (the low E and A) while your left hand stays in fifth position.

Track 58

Another One

26

You can use almost any of the songs in Book 1 to practice playing in 5th position, and this is probably the best way to really learn it. (Go ahead—the time you spend will be well worth it.)

When you think you know this position well enough, try some new songs, like these:

Track 59

Drunken Sailor

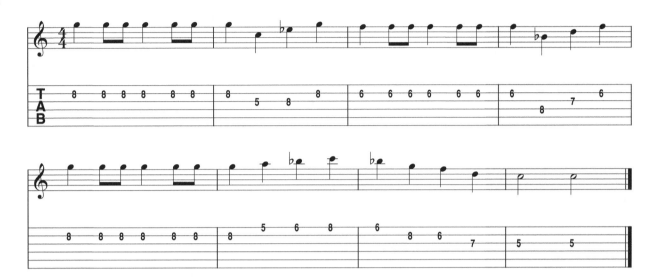

Track 60

The Yellow Rose of Texas

Take it slow and easy.

Track 61

Shenandoah

Changing Positions

Sometimes, you'll want to use more than one position to play a song—for instance, you might start a song in open position, then move up to fifth position for some higher notes, then move back down again. If you don't have TAB to show you the convenient positions, it's a good idea to survey the song before playing it, and mark the appropriate spots to change positions. Use Roman numerals (I and V) to mark these position changes.

Track 62

Arkansas Traveler

▶ If your strings "squeak" a bit as you move between positions, don't worry about it; try releasing your left-hand pressure as you move between positions.

Track 63

Rock-a-Bye

28

Barre Chords

Remember the barre technique we used in playing the F chord? This is actually a very common tool in guitar playing. In fact, we use it to form **movable barre chords**—major and minor chords that can be played anywhere along the neck using just a few simple shapes.

We'll learn four types of barre chords, based on four different open position chords: E, Em, A, and Am. But first, let's work on that barre. WARNING: This may be the most difficult technique you undertake as a beginning guitarist! The key to your ultimate success will be practice and patience.

The Full Barre
barre symbol

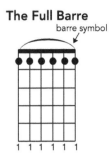

The Full Barre

The real trick to playing barre chords is being able to barre across all six strings of the guitar with just your index finger—*and* have each string sound clearly. So let's practice this first:

Step 1: Form a full barre by flattening your first finger across all six strings. Try this at the first fret.

Step 2: Support the barre by placing your thumb on the underside of the guitar neck, directly beneath your first finger. (Think of the thumb and index finger as a clamp that presses the neck together.)

Step 3: Strum all six strings. Readjust your finger, if necessary, until every string sounds clearly. HINT: It usually helps to turn your first finger slightly to the side when using it to barre.

The "Eight-Barre" Blues

E-Type Barre Chord

The first form that we'll learn is called the E-type barre chord, because it looks like an E chord. We'll use this E shape to play major chords up and down the sixth string.

Step 1: Play an open E major chord, but use your 2nd, 3rd, and 4th fingers. (That's right, this is a new fingering.)

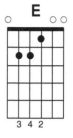

Step 2: Slide this chord shape up one fret, and add your 1st finger across the 1st fret, forming a barre.

Now, just strum all six strings, and voilà—your first barre chord! This particular barre chord is F major because its root is F on the sixth string. But you can apply this same shape to any root note along the sixth string:

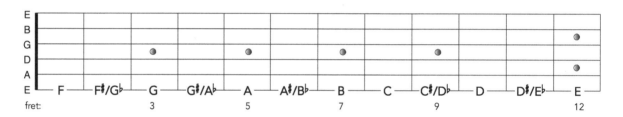

Most guitars have mother-of-pearl inlay markers on the fretboard to make it easier for you to find positions. The third, fifth, seventh, and ninth frets are commonly marked with a single inlay, while the twelfth fret is usually marked with a double inlay to indicate the octave position.

Track 66

Sweet Mother of Pearl!

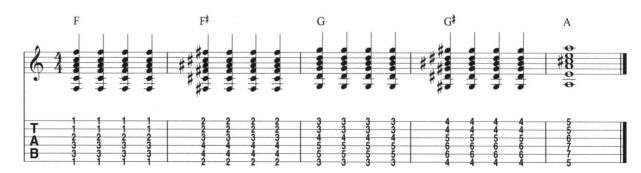

Let's try some riffs that move this shape around.

Track 67

Life's Good

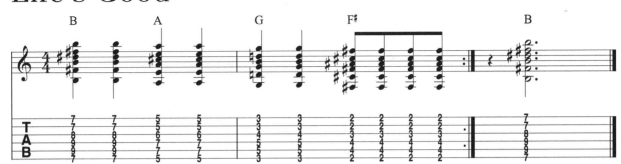

Track 68

Punkish

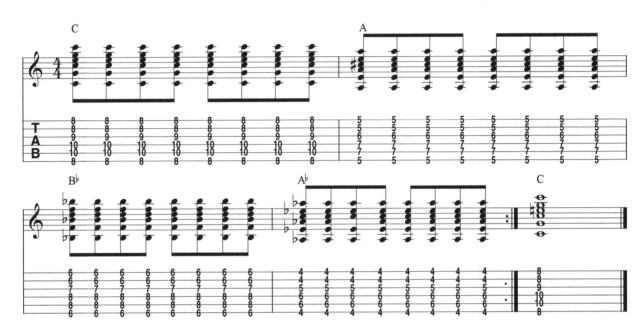

The "Thumb-and-Index" Barre

If you just can't get that index finger to barre across all six strings, here's a quick-and-dirty shortcut: Let your index finger barre just the top two strings, and allow your thumb to wrap around the top of the neck, fretting the sixth string. This works especially well on electric guitars.

WARNING: Even if you can do this alternate barre, don't stop working on your full barre! You'll be glad you did.

The Staccato Effect

Some songs are played with a short, bouncy articulation called staccato. This is indicated by a dot above the note or chord.

Track 69

To produce this sound, first play the chord as normal, then quickly release your left-hand pressure without losing contact with the strings.

The Percussion Effect, a.k.a. "Chord Scratch"

Taking this one step further, try strumming the strings while your left hand rests lightly against them. You should get a muted, percussive sound—indicated by an "x" in notation and TAB.

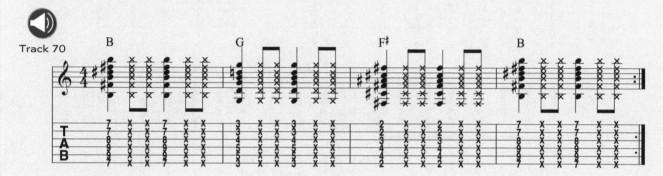

Track 70

You can use this technique to add rhythm to a song without producing any definite pitch.

The Way I Feel

Track 71

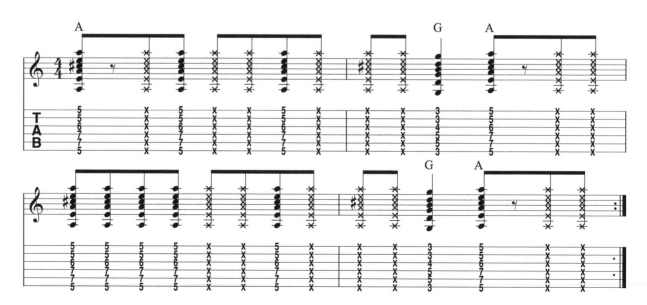

Em-Type Barre Chord

The same barring technique can be used for minor chords too. Since we used the E major shape for the major barre chords, we'll use the E minor shape for the minor barre chords along the sixth string.

Step 1: Play an open Em chord, using your 3rd and 4th fingers.

Em

Step 2: Slide the Em shape up one fret, and add a 1st finger barre across the 1st fret.

Fm

Voilà—an Fm barre chord! Now try switching between your major and minor barre chords. It's as easy as lifting a finger.

Track 72

From Major to Minor

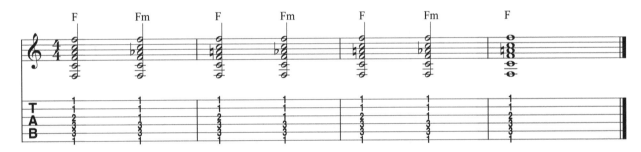

Track 73

Minor Vamp

33

Choosing the Best Chord Position

Although you should learn to play barre chords in all positions, in actual music, you'll often want to mix barre chords with open-position chords. Not only is this easier on the left hand, it adds more variety to your sound.

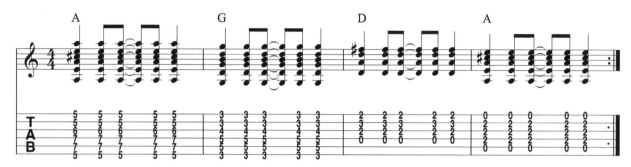

Some progressions are impossible to play without barre chords:

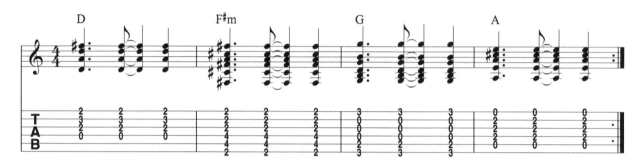

Others just sound better when played with barre chords:

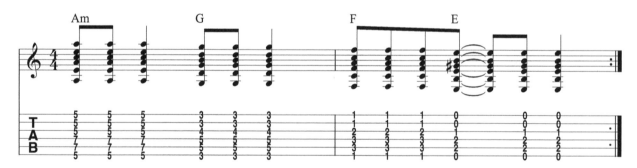

Still Having Trouble?

The easiest barre chords to play are those at the area of the fifth fret. However, with practice, your hand will become stronger, and you'll have less difficulty playing barre chords in any position. In the meantime, remember the following:

- Use just enough pressure on the strings to produce a clear tone.
- Always place your left thumb on the guitar neck *directly behind the barre* for additional support.
- When moving from one barre chord to another, keep your fingers in position and release pressure slightly, without losing contact with the strings.

Just as we converted the E and Em chord shapes into barre chords, we can do the same with A and Am chord shapes. These will have their roots on the fifth string.

A-Type Barre Chord

The formula is essentially the same: start with an open A chord, then move it up one fret and add a first-finger barre.

Open A chord shape...

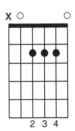

...converted barre chord shape

Instead of fretting each note individually for the A shape, try forming another barre with your third finger, as shown. Bend your third finger at the knuckle and lay it across strings 2-4. Once you get used to it, this fingering is a lot easier to move up and down the neck.

Am-Type Barre Chord

Once again: start with an open Am, move it up a fret and add the first-finger barre. Notice how this looks like the "E" type barre chord but moved over one string?

Open Am chord shape...

...converted barre chord shape

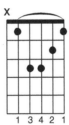

Practice these A-form barre chords up and down the neck. Remember: the root of these shapes lies along the fifth string:

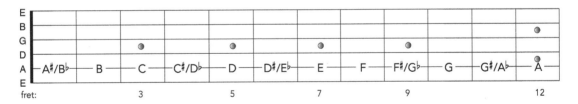

Strollin'

► Be patient; barre chords can take weeks or even months of practice.

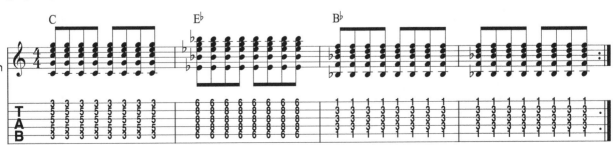

Battle Song

Track 76

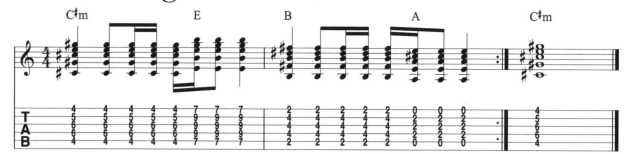

Love It or Leave It

Track 77

If you have difficulty playing the first string on the A form, just leave it out.

Four Shapes In All

It shouldn't take much movement to shift from E-form to A-form barre chords. The first finger can remain in place; then it's just a matter of moving fingers 2-4, or rolling the third finger into place.

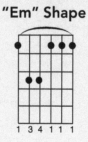

"E" Shape

1 3 4 2 1 1

"Em" Shape

1 3 4 1 1 1

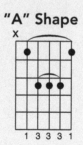

"A" Shape

1 3 3 3 1

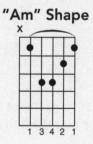

"Am" Shape

1 3 4 2 1

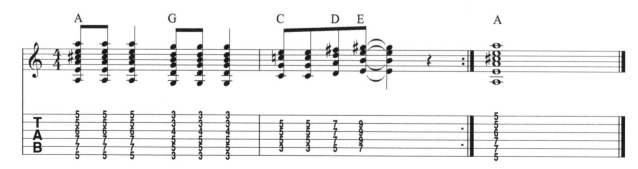

Song 1

Track 78

Tango

Track 79

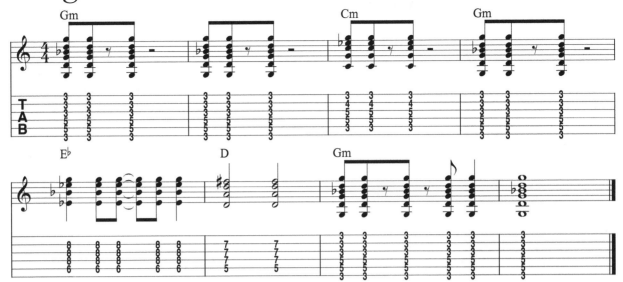

Feelin' Good

Track 80

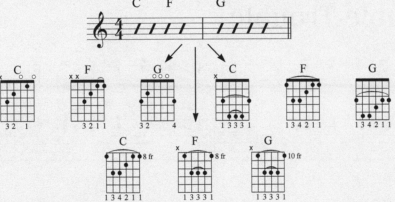

Choosing the Best Chord Position, Pt. 2

Using combinations of E-form and A-form barre chords—as well as open-position chords—can help you avoid large position jumps in your playing. For example, this chord progression could be played at least three ways:

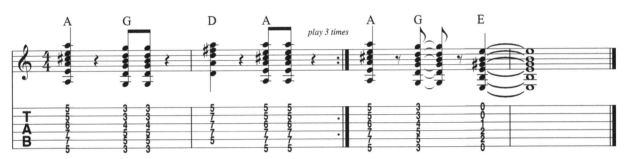

Before learning a song, play through the arrangement and select:

- the chords that sound best for each measure—open or barre.
- the chords that give you enough time to change positions.

When you have a choice of positions for the same chord:

- Use a chord position on a higher fret to produce a sharper, thinner sound.
- Use a chord position on a lower fret to produce a heavier, fuller sound.

37

Track 81

LESSON 8 | Slides, Hammer-Ons, Pull-Offs, and Bends

Sometimes, it's not so much what you play, it's how you play it. In music terms, this is called *articulation*. Slides, hammer-ons, pull-offs, and bends all belong to a special category of articulations called *legato*. Legato techniques allows you to "slur" two or more notes together to create a smooth, flowing sound.

With all of these techniques, you'll be playing one note as you normally would—with a pick held in your right hand. But the next note (the slurred one), you'll be articulating with your left hand only.

Slides

Pick the first note, then sound the second note by sliding the same left-hand finger up or down along the string. (The second note is not picked.)

The best way to practice this is in some riffs.

Track 82

► Use your first and third fingers for this first riff. (Your third finger will do the sliding.)

Smooth

Track 83

► Use an index-finger barre, or your ring and pinky fingers together, for this slide.

Double Trouble

Track 84

Slidin' Power

Hammer-Ons

Pick the first note, then tap, or "hammer on," to the higher note with another left-hand finger, along the same string. If you hammer too hard, your fingertips will hurt; too soft, and you won't hear anything. Keep practicing until you think you've got it.

Work It Out

Long Long Ago

► Hammer-ons can work for chords as well.

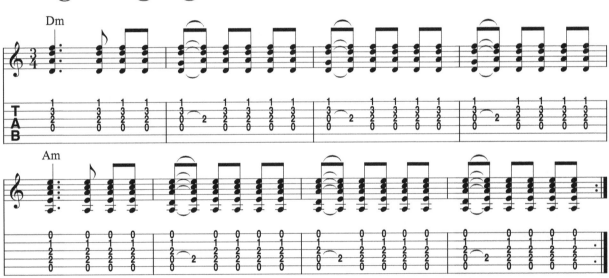

Pull-Offs

A pull-off is the opposite of a hammer-on. First, start with both fingers planted. Pick the higher note, then tug or "pull" that finger off the string to sound the lower note, already fretted by the lower finger.

Back and Forth

Push and Pull

Track 88

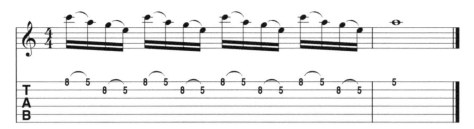

At the Roadhouse

Track 89

▶ Hammer-ons and pull-offs together make a popular combination.

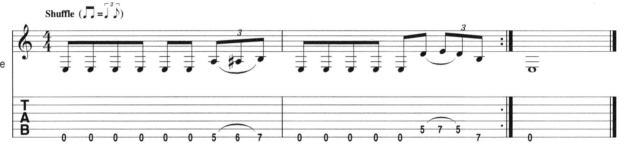

Bends

In general, bending is done on the first three strings, bending "up," or towards the ceiling. Most bends are either whole-step or half-step.

Whole-step bend

Pick the note indicated (D), then push the string upwards until it matches the sound of the target pitch (E), one whole step higher. (To check yourself, play E on fret 9 first.)

Half-step bend

Pick the note indicated (D), then push the string upwards, but not quite as high, to match the target pitch (E♭) one half step higher. (Check yourself with fret 8.)

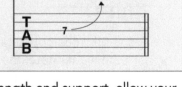

Bends are usually easiest when done with the third finger. For more strength and support, allow your first and second fingers to back up the third finger. This is called *reinforced bending*.

Bendin' Up

Track 90

▶ To get more leverage, don't forget to push down with your thumb on the back of the neck.

Up and Down

Track 91

► Once you've bent up, you may as well bring it back down.

Double Stops

Track 92

► Use your third and fourth fingers together for this double bend.

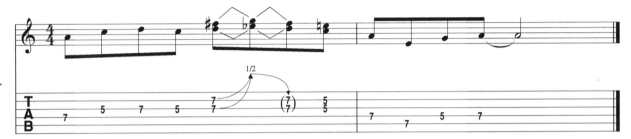

Of course, slides, hammer-ons, pull-offs, and bends can all be combined for some really cool licks.

Riff-a-Rama

Track 93

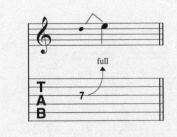

Grace-note bends differ from the other bends only in their rhythm—the first note (the one being bent) does not take up any time. Strike the first note (the grace note) with your pick, then immediately bend it upward to the next note.

Odds 'n' Ends

Minor Scales & Keys

As we mentioned previously, music can be based in both major and minor keys. Here are a few of the most commonly used minor scales:

Key of A minor

Key of E minor

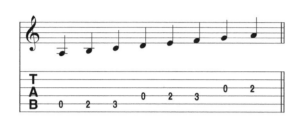

Key of D minor

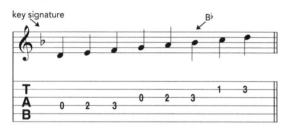

Notice anything familar about these key signatures? They're the same ones that we learned for C major, G major, and F major! That's because each of these is a *relative minor* of a major scale—containing the same notes, just played in a different order, with a different emphasis.

Am Riff

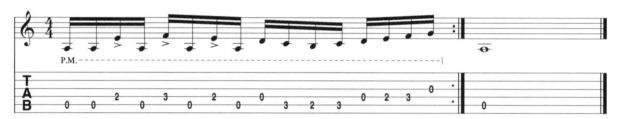

Em Riff

Dm Riff

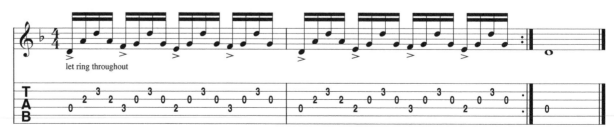

The I, IV, and V chords are important in all keys—including minor ones. However, in minor keys, these chords are typically minor (indicated with lower-case Roman numerals i, iv, v)—except for the "five" chord, which can be major (V) or dominant (V7).

Key	Chord / Scale Tone							
	i			**iv**	**v or V**			
A minor	Am	B	C	Dm	Em or E	F	G	A
D minor	Dm	E	F	Gm	Am or A	B♭	C	D
E minor	Em	F♯	G	Am	Bm or B	C	D	E

i-iv-V

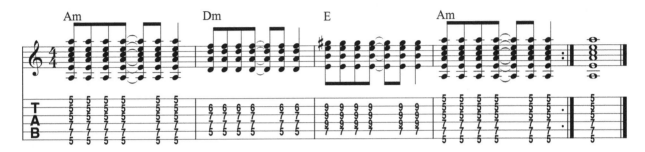

Just because i, iv, and V are important doesn't mean you can't use other chords.

Other Chords

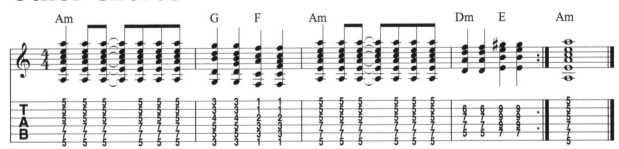

The Circle of Fifths

The *circle of fifths* is a useful tool if you want to know what chords are available within a key. Major keys line the ouside of the circle; their relative minors line the inside.

Right now, the box is highlighting chords that belong to both C major and its relative A minor—that is, F, C, G, Dm, Am, Em. To find the chords for another key, just mentally rotate the box.

For example, if a song contains the chords D, A, E, and Bm, what key is it in?

Answer: A major!

Dominant Seventh Barre Chords

Here are a few barre chord voicings for dominant sevenths. The E7-type works anywhere along the sixth string; the A7-type, anywhere along the fifth string.

Open E7 chord shape...

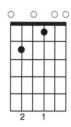

...converted barre chord shape

Open A7 chord shape...

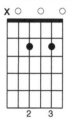

...converted barre chord shape

Mustang Sarah

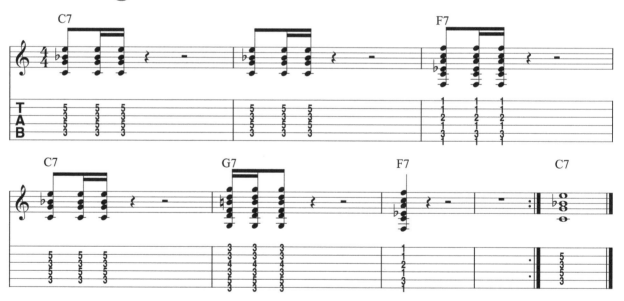

How Sweet It Is

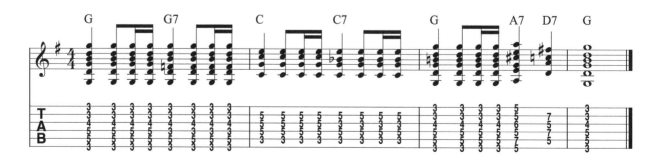

Track 95

44

Track 96

Movable Scale Forms

Like power chords and barre chords, scales are easier to use if they are movable—that way, a few shapes moved up and down the neck allow you to play in any key. We already learned one movable scale form—the "blues" scale; here are two more essential patterns:

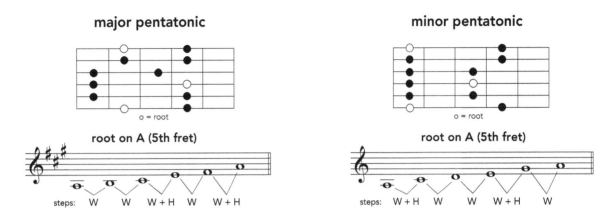

These are actually just simplified versions of the major and minor scales we already learned, with just five notes in each octave instead of seven. (The prefix *penta-* means "five.") With fewer notes, these scales have a smoother, more streamlined sound, making them especially good for improvising.

Major Pentatonic

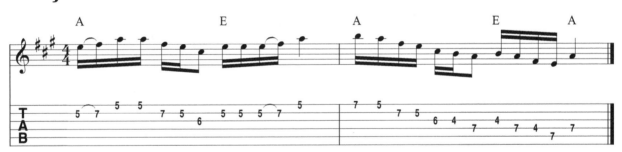

Minor Pentatonic

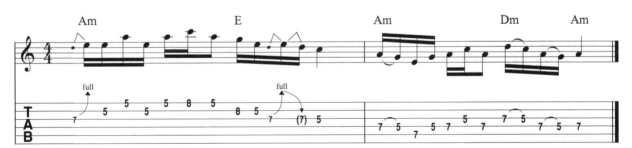

In general, try playing the major pentatonic scale over songs in major keys; the minor pentatonic over songs in minor keys. Use a song's key signature or its chord progression to help you determine its key.

45

Unusual Chords

Here are some less common open-position chords to wrap your fingers around. These are good fun to practice when you need a break from barre chords. Generally speaking, you can substitute these for the more common open position major chords.

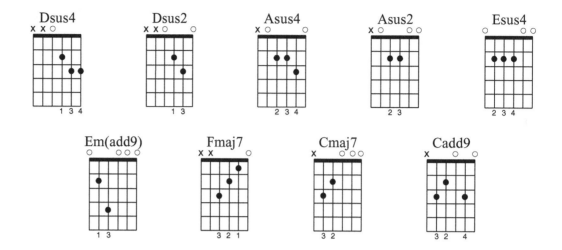

Inspiration

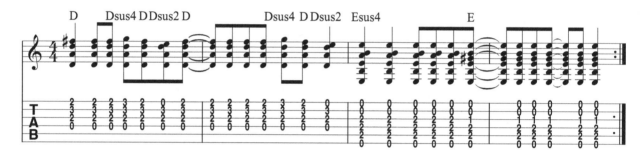

Open Strumming

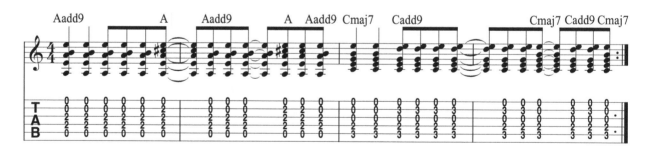

As you've no doubt noticed, these aren't too different from the major shapes we've already learned. Feel free to develop your own chords by taking an existing shape and changing a note here and there, and see what you come up with.

Track 98

Three-Note Chord Forms

Finally, here's one more antidote to "barre chord"-itis. These three-note shapes are all movable—just like barre chords—but they're much easier to play. Being on the top three strings, they also have a thin, cutting sound which makes them ideal for some rhythm guitar styles.

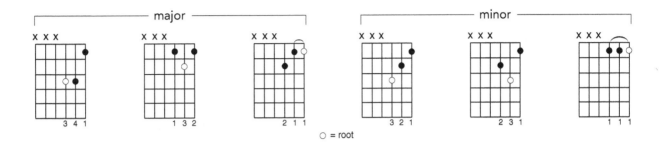

○ = root

Pay attention to the root in each voicing; it tells you what chord you are playing. (The root will be on one of the top three strings—not necessarily on the bottom.)

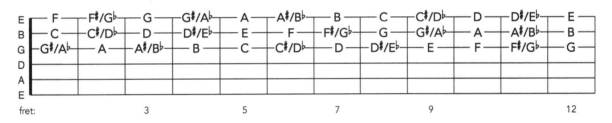

Reggae

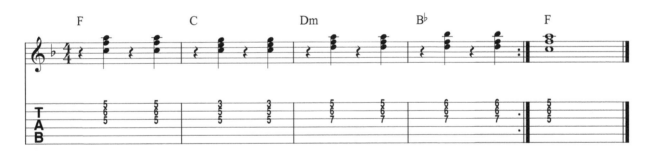

Fragments

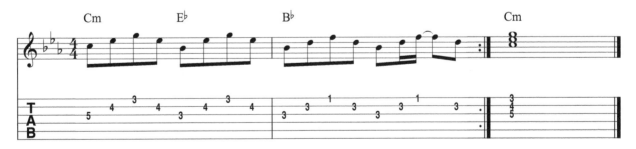

47

Review
Notes on the Fretboard

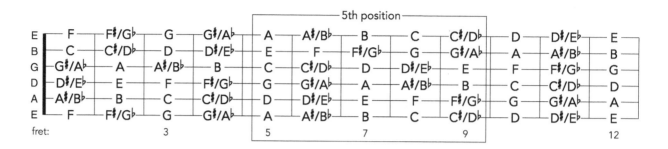

Notes in Fifth Position

Chords and Shapes

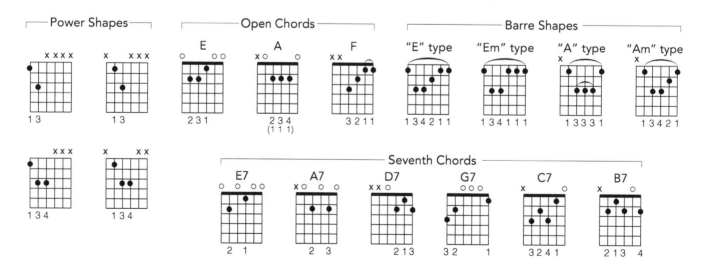